The Essential Ninja Double Stack Air Fryer

Cookbook for Beginners

Tastefully Delicious, Simple and Easy to follow Recipes for Healthy, Crispy Meals. Perfect for Large Families.

Katherine Lawrence

Copyright notice

PREFACE

Hello there,

Welcome to the "Zero Point Family Weight Loss Cookbook: Healthy and Delicious Recipes for Parents and Kids"! We are thrilled to embark on this wonderful journey of family recipes with you, where we transform everyday meals into nutritious, zero point delights that the whole family can enjoy. This cookbook is designed with you in mind—busy parents who want to provide healthy, tasty, and simple meals for their children without spending endless hours in the kitchen.

Our goal is to make healthy eating accessible, enjoyable, and sustainable for families. We understand the challenges that come with balancing work, school, and extracurricular activities, all while trying to maintain a healthy lifestyle. This is why we have compiled a collection of recipes that are not only zero point but also quick, easy, and kid-friendly.

We believe that eating healthy shouldn't be a chore. Instead, it should be a fun and rewarding experience that brings the family together. In this cookbook, you'll find a variety of meals that cater to different tastes and preferences, ensuring that everyone in your family can find something they love. From energizing breakfasts to hearty dinners, delightful snacks to indulgent desserts, we've got you covered.

Thank you for choosing our cookbook as your guide to healthier family meals. We hope that these recipes inspire you to create delicious, zero point dishes that your family will love. Here's to happy, healthy cooking and eating!

To a healthier you,

Katherine Lawrence
AUTHOR

TABLE OF CONTENTS

Welcome to the Ninja Double Stack Cookbook

I already know what you may be thinking, so let me explain. What sets this cookbook apart from the competition is that it was created especially for the Ninja Double Stack Air Fryer and has mouthwatering recipes that can be cooked to perfection with Air fryer technology.

With the Ninja Double Stack Air Fryer Cookbook, welcome to the world of inventive and convenient cooking! This cookbook is meant for people who are enthusiastic about cooking with the Ninja Double Stack Air fryer, who like tasty, home-cooked meals without any hassle, or even for those who have never used one before.

A really innovative kitchen tool, the Ninja Double Stack Air Fryer enhances your culinary routine with its adaptability, effectiveness, and health advantages. This guidebook will lead you through a variety of delicious (tried and tested by me) dishes, from decadent sweet delicacies to mouthwatering breakfasts, all designed to make your time using the Ninja Double Stack Air Fryer a truly delightful one.

In addition to offering you recipes, this cookbook hopes to encourage experimentation and a love of cooking. With its innovative dual-basket design, the Ninja Double Stack Air Fryer creates endless possibilities for cooking numerous foods at once or easily preparing big batches. The recipes in this book will satisfy all of your needs and tastes, whether you're cooking for the family or just seeking for quick and healthful supper ideas.

The Advantages of Using a Double Stack Ninja

The Ninja Double Stack Air Fryer has the potential to completely transform your life; it's not simply another kitchen tool. Here are a few main advantages I've discovered from utilising this appliance:

1. **Healthier Cooking**: You may cook with little to no oil thanks to air fry technology, which drastically lowers the fat level of your food. This implies that you can indulge in your favourite fried meals guilt-free, such doughnuts, chicken wings, and chips.

2. **Versatility**: Air frying is not the only use for the Ninja Double Stack Air Fryer. It is an adaptable kitchen gadget that can also bake, roast, reheat, and dehydrate. With just one appliance, you may make a broad variety of foods, such as baked pastries, dehydrated fruits, roasted vegetables, and warmed leftovers.

3. **Time-saving**: You can cook two separate foods at once with the dual-basket design, which will help you save valuable time in the kitchen. Multitasking is a breeze with the Ninja Double

Here are some pointers to get you started and help you get the most out of your Ninja Double Stack Air Fryer if you've never used one before:

Stack Air Fryer, whether you're cooking for a big crowd or preparing a main course and a side dish.

4. **Energy Efficiency**: The Ninja Double Stack Air Fryer uses less energy than conventional ovens because of its small size and quick cooking process. This lowers your carbon impact in addition to saving you money on energy expenses.

5. **Reliable Outcomes**: The Ninja Double Stack Air Fryer guarantees reliable outcomes and even frying every time. Food is cooked uniformly by the hot air that circulates, reducing the possibility of undercooked or burned areas. This implies that you can work less and still get flawless outcomes.

6. **Easy to Clean**: Cleaning is a joy because to the detachable baskets and non-stick surfaces. You may spend more time enjoying your meals and less time scrubbing because the majority of the parts are dishwasher safe.

1. **Read the Manual**: Spend some time reading the user manual for your air fryer before using it. You can operate the appliance more efficiently and safely if you are aware of its features, settings, and safety measures.

2. **Preheat the Air Fryer:** Heating your air fryer before adding food will help you get better results, just like in a regular oven. A crispier texture and more even cooking result from preheating since it guarantees that the food cooks instantly.

3. **Don't Overcrowd the Baskets**: Try not to fill the baskets to the brim for optimal outcomes. To ensure that everything cooks evenly, leave some room around the meal so that hot air may circulate. Think about cooking a large amount in many smaller batches if necessary.

4. **Shake or Turn Food**: It is a good idea to shake or turn foods midway through the cooking process, such as chips or chicken wings, that

require even browning. This aids in producing a consistent golden-brown crust around the edges.

5. **Use a Light Oil Spray**: Although the air fryer uses very little to no oil, some foods will crisp up more if you use a light oil spray. Before cooking, lightly coat the item in oil using a spray bottle.

6. **Experiment with Cooking Times**: Depending on the kind and quantity of food you are cooking, cooking times can change. To get the right results, don't be scared to experiment and change the cooking times. For future reference, start with the suggested timings and record any changes.

7. **Use the Right Accessories:** You can cook a wider variety of foods in your Ninja Double Stack Air Fryer by investing in a few air fryer accessories, such as silicone baking cups, cake pans, and grill racks. These add-ons are made to be both temperature-resistant and precisely fit within the baskets.

8. **Clean Often:** You should clean your air fryer frequently to preserve its longevity and functionality. After every usage, remove and clean the trays and baskets, then use a damp cloth to wipe off the exterior and interior.

Crucial Instruments and Attachments

Think about spending money on a few necessary tools and accessories to get the most out of your Ninja Double Stack Air Fryer. These will improve your culinary skills and enable you to make a greater range of dishes. Here are a few essentials:

1. **Silicone Baking Cups**: These reusable, non-stick baking cups are ideal for preparing muffins, cupcakes, and individual quiches.

2. **Cake Pan**: For baking cakes, bread, and other baked goods, a tiny cake pan that fits in the air fryer basket works wonderfully. Seek for cookware composed of materials resistant to elevated temperatures.

3. **Grill Rack**: By raising the food, you may encourage uniform browning and air circulation. It's perfect for grilling seafood, veggies, and meats.

4. **Perforated Parchment Paper**: This paper makes cleanup easier by keeping food from adhering to the basket. The holes facilitate the circulation of hot air, guaranteeing uniform cooking.

5. **Oil Spray Bottle**: For softly smearing oil over food, a reusable oil spray bottle comes in helpful. By doing this, you may get a crispy texture without using a lot of oil.

6. **Kitchen Tongs:** To turn and remove food from the air fryer baskets, you'll need a pair of heat-resistant kitchen tongs. In order to prevent scratching the non-stick surfaces, look for tongs with silicone tips.

7. **Meat Thermometer:** A meat thermometer is a helpful tool for making sure that meats are cooked to the right internal temperature. By doing this, overcooking or undercooking is prevented.

Best Practices and Safety Advice

When utilising any kitchen gadget, safety must always come first. The following are some recommended practices and safety advice to remember when using your Ninja Double Stack Air Fryer:

1. **Read the Manual**: Become acquainted with the user manual and adhere to the safety recommendations and manufacturer's instructions.

2. **Position on a sturdy Surface**: To avoid the air fryer toppling over, make sure it is positioned on a level, sturdy surface that is not close to the countertop's edge.

3. **Prevent Vent Blocking:** Keep the air fryer's vents clear. For operations to be both safe and effective, proper ventilation is necessary.

4. **Put on oven mitts**: When cooking, the baskets and accessories might get extremely hot. To handle them safely, put on oven mitts or heat-resistant gloves.

5. **Unplug When Not in Use**: Unplug the air fryer when cleaning or not in use to avoid electrical dangers.

6. **Keep Away from Water**: To reduce the chance of electric shock, keep the air fryer away from liquids or water.

7. **Avoid Overfilling:** When baskets are overfilled, air circulation is impeded, which can cause uneven cooking. For optimal results, adhere to the suggested maximum fill levels.

8. **Watch the Cooking Process**: Pay close attention to the cooking process, particularly when experimenting with new recipes. As necessary, modify the cooking duration and temperature to avoid burning or overcooking.

9. **Let Cool**: Prior to cleaning, let the air fryer cool all the way down. By doing this, you may handle the parts safely and avoid burns.

10. **Routine Maintenance**: Conduct routine maintenance, such as checking the condition of the trays and baskets and looking for damage on the power cable.

You can cook great meals for your family and yourself with your Ninja Double Stack Air Fryer in a safe and efficient manner according to these best practices and guidelines. Have fun in the kitchen!

contribute to meeting your daily nutritional needs without adding unnecessary calories.

Satiating: Many zero point foods are high in fiber and protein, which help you feel fuller for longer. This can help control hunger and prevent overeating.

Natural and Unprocessed: Most zero point foods are whole, unprocessed items such as fruits, vegetables, lean proteins, and legumes. These foods are closer to their natural state, providing more nutritional benefits.

How Zero Point Foods Are Determined

Zero point foods are typically chosen based on their nutritional profile and their ability to contribute to a healthy diet without excessive calorie intake. These foods are often:

Low in Fat and Sugar: Foods that are low in unhealthy fats and added sugars are prioritized, as they are less likely to contribute to weight gain and other health issues.

High in Fiber and Protein: Foods that are high in fiber and protein help promote satiety and provide essential nutrients for maintaining muscle mass and overall health.

Nutrient-Rich: Foods that are packed with vitamins, minerals, and antioxidants are chosen for their health benefits.

How to Incorporate Zero Point Foods into Family Meals

Incorporating zero point foods into your family meals can be both easy and enjoyable. Here are some practical tips and ideas for making zero point foods a regular part of your family's diet:

Meal Planning with Zero Point Foods

1. **Start with a Plan**
Weekly Menu: Plan your meals for the week, including breakfast, lunch, dinner, and snacks. Make sure to include a variety of zero point foods in each meal.

Grocery List: Create a grocery list based on your meal plan, focusing on zero point foods. This helps ensure you have all the necessary ingredients on hand.

2. **Batch Cooking**
Prepare in Bulk: Cook large batches of zero point foods, such as grilled chicken breast, roasted vegetables, and quinoa, and store them in the refrigerator or freezer for easy access throughout the week.

Portion Control: Divide batch-cooked foods into individual portions to make meal prep easier and to help manage portion sizes.

3. **Incorporate Variety**

Mix and Match: Combine different zero point foods to create a variety of meals. For example, mix different vegetables for a stir-fry or combine various fruits for a fruit salad.
Seasonal Choices: Choose seasonal fruits and vegetables to add variety and take advantage of their peak flavor and nutritional value.

Breakfast Recipes

Serves: 1

Ingredients:
- 2 sausages
- 2 rashers of bacon
- 1 tomato, halved
- 1 mushroom, halved
- 1 slice of black pudding
- 1 egg
- 100g baked beans
- 1 slice of toast
- Salt and pepper to taste

Cooking Time: - 24 minutes

Instructions:
1. Preheat the air fryer to 180°C.
2. Place the sausages in one basket and cook for 10 minutes.
3. Add the bacon, tomato, mushroom, and black pudding to the other basket. Cook for 8 minutes, turning halfway through.
4. Crack the egg into a small, air fryer-safe dish and place it in the basket with the bacon. Cook for an additional 6 minutes or until the egg is cooked to your liking.
5. Heat the baked beans in a small pan or microwave.
6. Toast the bread.
7. Serve everything on a plate, season with salt and pepper, and enjoy.

Nutritional Information:
- **Calories: 850**
- **Protein: 40g**
- **Fat: 60g**
- **Carbohydrates: 40g**
- **Fibre: 10g**

Serves: - Makes about 8 pancakes

Ingredients:
- 200g self-raising flour
- 50g caster sugar
- 2 large eggs
- 200ml milk
- A pinch of salt
- Butter or oil for greasing

Cook Time: 10 minutes

Instructions:
1. Preheat the air fryer to 160°C.
2. In a bowl, mix the flour, sugar, and salt.
3. Beat the eggs and milk together, then gradually whisk into the dry ingredients to form a smooth batter.
4. Lightly grease the air fryer basket or use a silicone baking mat.
5. Drop spoonfuls of batter into the basket, forming small pancakes.
6. Cook for 5 minutes on each side or until golden brown and cooked through.
7. Serve warm with butter, syrup, or your favourite toppings.

Nutritional Information:
- **Calories: 120**
- **Protein: 3g**
- **Fat: 2g**
- **Carbohydrates: 22g**
- **Fibre: 1g**

Serves: 4

Ingredients:
- 4 English muffins, halved
- 8 slices of bacon
- 4 eggs
- 100g cheddar cheese, grated
- Salt and pepper to taste

Cooking Time: - - 16 minutes

Instructions:
1. Preheat the air fryer to 180°C.
2. Place the bacon in one basket and cook for 8 minutes, turning halfway through.
3. While the bacon is cooking, toast the muffin halves in the other basket for 3-4 minutes.
4. In an air fryer-safe dish, cook the eggs to your liking (fried or scrambled) for 6-8 minutes.
5. Assemble the muffins by placing bacon, egg, and cheese on each muffin half.
6. Return the assembled muffins to the air fryer for 2-3 minutes to melt the cheese.
7. Season with salt and pepper and serve warm.

Nutritional Information:
- **Calories: 300**
- **Protein: 18g**
- **Fat: 15g**
- **Carbohydrates: 25g**
- **Fibre: 2g**

Air Fryer Hash Browns

- Makes 4 hash browns

Ingredients:
- 2 large potatoes, peeled and grated
- 1 small onion, grated
- 1 egg
- 2 tbsp plain flour
- Salt and pepper to taste
- Olive oil spray

Cook Time: - 12 minutes

Instructions:
1. Preheat the air fryer to 180°C.
2. Squeeze out excess moisture from the grated potatoes and onion using a clean kitchen towel.
3. In a bowl, mix the grated potatoes, onion, egg, flour, salt, and pepper.
4. Form the mixture into small patties.
5. Spray the air fryer basket with olive oil and place the patties inside.
6. Cook for 10-12 minutes, turning halfway through, until golden brown and crispy.
7. Serve hot with your favourite breakfast accompaniments.

Nutritional Information:
- **Calories: 100**
- **Protein: 3g**
- **Fat: 3g**
- **Carbohydrates: 15g**
- **Fibre: 2g**

Serves: 4

Ingredients:
- 6 large eggs
- 100ml milk
- 1 red pepper, diced
- 1 courgette, grated
- 1 small onion, finely chopped
- 50g spinach, chopped
- 50g feta cheese, crumbled
- Salt and pepper to taste

Cooking Time: - 18 minutes

Instructions:
1. Preheat the air fryer to 180°C.
2. In a large bowl, whisk together the eggs and milk. Season with salt and pepper.
3. Stir in the red pepper, courgette, onion, and spinach.
4. Pour the mixture into an air fryer-safe dish.
5. Sprinkle the feta cheese on top.
6. Cook in the air fryer for 15-18 minutes, or until the frittata is set and golden brown.
7. Slice and serve warm.

Nutritional Information:
- **Calories: 200**
- **Protein: 12g**
- **Fat: 12g**
- **Carbohydrates: 8g**
- **Fibre: 2g**

Sausage and Egg Breakfast Sandwiches

Serves 4

Ingredients:
- 4 sausage patties
- 4 eggs
- 4 slices of cheese
- 4 English muffins, halved
- Salt and pepper to taste

Cook Time: - 16 minutes

Instructions:
1. Preheat the air fryer to 180°C.
2. Cook the sausage patties in one basket for 8-10 minutes, turning halfway through.
3. While the sausages are cooking, toast the muffin halves in the other basket for 3-4 minutes.
4. In an air fryer-safe dish, cook the eggs to your liking (fried or scrambled) for 6-8 minutes.
5. Assemble the sandwiches by placing a sausage patty, egg, and cheese slice on each muffin half.
6. Return the assembled sandwiches to the air fryer for 2-3 minutes to melt the cheese.
7. Season with salt and pepper and serve warm.

Nutritional Information:
- **Calories: 400**
- **Protein: 20g**
- **Fat: 25g**
- **Carbohydrates: 25g**
- **Fibre: 2g**

Cinnamon Rolls

Serves: Makes 8-10 rolls

Ingredients:
- 250g plain flour
- 50g caster sugar
- 1 packet (7g) instant yeast
- 125ml warm milk
- 50g butter, melted
- 1 egg
- 1 tsp ground cinnamon
- 75g brown sugar
- 25g butter, softened

Cooking Time: - 15 minutes

Instructions:
1. Preheat the air fryer to 180°C.
2. In a bowl, combine the flour, caster sugar, and yeast.
3. Add the warm milk, melted butter, and egg, and mix to form a dough.
4. Knead the dough for 5-10 minutes, then let it rise in a warm place for 1 hour or until doubled in size.
5. Roll out the dough into a rectangle.
6. Mix the ground cinnamon and brown sugar together, then spread the softened butter over the dough and sprinkle with the cinnamon sugar mixture.
7. Roll up the dough tightly and cut into 8-10 rolls.
8. Place the rolls in the air fryer basket and cook for 12-15 minutes, or until golden brown.
9. Allow to cool slightly before serving.

Nutritional Information:
- **Calories: 250**
- **Protein: 5g**
- **Fat: 10g**
- **Carbohydrates: 35g**
- **Fibre: 2g**

Air Fryer Porridge with Berries

Serves 2

Ingredients:
- 100g porridge oats
- 500ml milk or water
- 1 tbsp honey or maple syrup
- 100g mixed berries
- A pinch of salt

Cook Time: - 12 minutes

Instructions:
1. Preheat the air fryer to 160°C.
2. In an air fryer-safe dish, combine the porridge oats, milk or water, and a pinch of salt.
3. Cook for 10-12 minutes, stirring halfway through, until the oats are soft and creamy.
4. Stir in the honey or maple syrup.
5. Top with mixed berries and serve warm.

Nutritional Information:
- **Calories: 200**
- **Protein: 8g**
- **Fat: 5g**
- **Carbohydrates: 35g**
- **Fibre: 5g**

Serves: 1

Ingredients:
- 200g baked beans
- 2 slices of bread
- Butter for spreading
- Salt and pepper to taste

Cooking Time: - 4 minutes

Instructions:
1. Preheat the air fryer to 180°C.
2. Toast the bread slices in the air fryer for 3-4 minutes, or until golden brown.
3. While the bread is toasting, heat the baked beans in a small pan or microwave.
4. Spread butter on the toasted bread and top with the baked beans.
5. Season with salt and pepper and serve immediately.

Nutritional Information:
- **Calories: 350**
- **Protein: 12g**
- **Fat: 10g**
- **Carbohydrates: 50g**
- **Fibre: 10g**

Makes 6 crumpets

Ingredients:
- 300g strong white bread flour
- 1 tsp salt
- 1 tsp caster sugar
- 1 tsp baking powder
- 300ml warm milk
- 100ml warm water
- 1 tsp dried yeast

Cook Time: - 12 minutes

Instructions:
1. Preheat the air fryer to 180°C.
2. In a bowl, mix the flour, salt, sugar, and baking powder.
3. In another bowl, combine the warm milk, water, and yeast. Let it sit for 5 minutes until frothy.
4. Pour the yeast mixture into the dry ingredients and mix to form a batter.
5. Cover and let the batter rise in a warm place for 1 hour.
6. Grease crumpet rings and place them in the air fryer basket.
7. Pour the batter into the rings and cook for 10-12 minutes, until the crumpets are golden brown and cooked through.
8. Serve warm with butter and jam.

Nutritional Information:
- **Calories: 120**
- **Protein: 4g**
- **Fat: 2g**
- **Carbohydrates: 22g**
- **Fibre: 1g**

- Makes 12 mini sausage rolls

Ingredients:
- 500g sausage meat
- 1 sheet of puff pastry
- 1 egg, beaten
- Salt and pepper to taste
- 1 tsp dried thyme (optional)

Cooking Time: 15 minutes

Instructions:
1. Preheat the air fryer to 180°C.
2. Roll out the puff pastry sheet and cut it into 2 long rectangles.
3. Mix the sausage meat with salt, pepper, and thyme (if using).
4. Place the sausage meat along the centre of each pastry rectangle.
5. Brush the edges with beaten egg, fold the pastry over the sausage meat, and press to seal.
6. Cut each long roll into mini sausage rolls.
7. Place the rolls in the air fryer basket and brush the tops with beaten egg.
8. Cook for 12-15 minutes, or until golden brown and cooked through.
9. Serve warm or cold.

Nutritional Information:
- **Calories: 150**
- **Protein: 5g**
- **Fat: 10g**
- **Carbohydrates: 12g**
- **Fibre: 1g**

Air Fryer Scotch Eggs

Serves: 4

Ingredients:
- 4 eggs, boiled and peeled
- 400g sausage meat
- 1 egg, beaten
- 100g breadcrumbs
- Salt and pepper to taste

Cooking Time: 15 minutes

Instructions:
1. Preheat the air fryer to 180°C.
2. Wrap each boiled egg in sausage meat, ensuring it is evenly coated.
3. Dip each sausage-coated egg into the beaten egg, then roll in breadcrumbs to coat.
4. Place the Scotch eggs in the air fryer basket.
5. Cook for 12-15 minutes, or until the sausage meat is cooked through and the coating is golden brown.
6. Serve warm or cold.

Nutritional Information:
- **Calories: 350**
- **Protein: 18g**
- **Fat: 25g**
- **Carbohydrates: 15g**
- **Fibre: 2g**

Makes 4 pasties

Ingredients:
- 1 sheet of puff pastry
- 200g cheddar cheese, grated
- 1 onion, finely chopped
- 1 egg, beaten
- Salt and pepper to taste

Cooking Time: 12 minutes

Instructions:

1. Preheat the air fryer to 180°C.
2. Roll out the puff pastry and cut into 4 squares.
3. Mix the grated cheese and chopped onion in a bowl. Season with salt and pepper.
4. Place a spoonful of the cheese and onion mixture in the centre of each pastry square.
5. Fold the pastry over to form a triangle and press the edges to seal.
6. Brush the tops with beaten egg.
7. Place the pasties in the air fryer basket.
8. Cook for 10-12 minutes, or until golden brown and crispy.

Nutritional Information:
- **Calories: 300**
- **Protein: 10g**
- **Fat: 20g**
- **Carbohydrates: 25g**
- **Fibre: 2g**

Makes 10 bon bons

Ingredients:
- 200g haggis
- 1 egg, beaten
- 100g breadcrumbs
- Oil spray

Cooking Time: - 12 minutes

Instructions:

1. Preheat the air fryer to 180°C.
2. Roll the haggis into small balls.
3. Dip each ball into the beaten egg, then roll in breadcrumbs to coat.
4. Place the bon bons in the air fryer basket and lightly spray with oil.
5. Cook for 10-12 minutes, or until golden brown and crispy.
6. Serve warm with a dipping sauce.

Nutritional Information:
- **-- Calories: 80**
- **Protein: 3g**
- **Fat: 4g**
- **Carbohydrates: 8g**
- **Fibre: 1g**

- Makes 8 fritters

Ingredients:
- 200g mushy peas
- 100g self-raising flour
- 1 egg
- Salt and pepper to taste
- Oil spray

Cooking Time: 12 minutes

Instructions:
1. Preheat the air fryer to 180°C.
2. In a bowl, mix the mushy peas, flour, and egg. Season with salt and pepper.
3. Form the mixture into small patties.
4. Place the patties in the air fryer basket and lightly spray with oil.
5. Cook for 10-12 minutes, or until golden brown and crispy, turning halfway through.
6. Serve warm.

Nutritional Information:
- **-- Calories: 60**
- **Protein: 2g**
- **Fat: 1g**
- **Carbohydrates: 10g**
- **Fibre: 2g**

Stuffed Mushrooms

Serves 4

Ingredients:
- 8 large mushrooms, stems removed
- 100g cream cheese
- 50g breadcrumbs
- 1 clove garlic, minced
- 2 tbsp parsley, chopped
- Salt and pepper to taste

Cooking Time: - 10 minutes

Instructions:
1. Preheat the air fryer to 180°C.
2. In a bowl, mix the cream cheese, breadcrumbs, garlic, parsley, salt, and pepper.
3. Stuff the cream cheese mixture into each mushroom cap.
4. Insert the stuffed mushrooms into the basket of the air fryer.
5. Cook for 8-10 minutes, or until the mushrooms are tender and the tops are golden brown.
6. Serve warm.

Nutritional Information:
- **Calories: 100**
- **Protein: 4g**
- **Fat: 8g**
- **Carbohydrates: 5g**
- **Fibre: 1g**

Makes 16 bites

Ingredients:
- 100g cheddar cheese, grated
- 1 tbsp butter
- 1 tbsp plain flour
- 50ml milk
- 1 tsp mustard
- 1 tsp Worcestershire sauce
- 4 slices of bread, cut into small squares

Cooking Time: 7 minutes

Instructions:
1. Preheat the air fryer to 180°C.
2. In a saucepan, melt the butter and stir in the flour to form a roux.
3. Gradually add the milk, stirring continuously until smooth and thickened.
4. Add the grated cheese, mustard, and Worcestershire sauce, and stir until melted and combined.
5. Spoon the cheese mixture onto the bread squares.
6. Place the bread squares in the air fryer basket.
7. Cook for 5-7 minutes, or until the cheese is bubbling and golden brown.
8. Serve warm.

Nutritional Information:
- **Calories: 60**
- **Protein: 3g**
- **Fat: 4g**
- **Carbohydrates: 4g**
- **Fibre: 0.5g**

- Makes 8 spring rolls

Ingredients:
- 8 spring roll wrappers
- 100g cooked chicken, shredded
- 50g bean sprouts
- 1 carrot, julienned
- 50g cabbage, shredded
- 1 tbsp soy sauce
- 1 tbsp hoisin sauce
- Oil spray

Cooking Time: - 12 minutes

Instructions:
1. Preheat the air fryer to 180°C.
2. In a bowl, mix the chicken, bean sprouts, carrot, cabbage, soy sauce, and hoisin sauce.
3. Place a spoonful of the mixture onto each spring roll wrapper and roll up, sealing the edges with a little water.
4. Place the spring rolls in the air fryer basket and lightly spray with oil.
5. Cook for 10-12 minutes, or until golden brown and crispy, turning halfway through.
6. Serve warm with dipping sauce.

Nutritional Information:
- **Calories: 100**
- **Protein: 5g**
- **Fat: 3g**
- **Carbohydrates: 12g**
- **Fibre: 2g**

Makes 16 bites

Ingredients:
- 8 vol-au-vent cases
- 100g cooked prawns, chopped
- 2 tbsp mayonnaise
- 1 tbsp ketchup
- 1 tsp lemon juice
- Salt and pepper to taste
- 1 tbsp chopped chives

Cooking Time: 7 minutes

Instructions:
1. Preheat the air fryer to 180°C.
2. In a bowl, mix the prawns, mayonnaise, ketchup, lemon juice, salt, and pepper.
3. Spoon the prawn mixture into the vol-au-vent cases.
4. Place the vol-au-vent cases in the air fryer basket.
5. Cook for 5-7 minutes, or until the cases are golden brown and the filling is heated through.
6. Garnish with chopped chives and serve warm.

Nutritional Information:
- **Calories: 70**
- **Protein: 4g**
- **Fat: 5g**
- **Carbohydrates: 5g**
- **Fibre: 0.5g**

Black Pudding Croquettes

Makes 8 croquettes

Ingredients:
- 200g black pudding, crumbled
- 100g mashed potatoes
- 1 egg, beaten
- 100g breadcrumbs
- Oil spray

Cooking Time: - 12 minutes

Instructions:
1. Preheat the air fryer to 180°C.
2. In a bowl, mix the crumbled black pudding and mashed potatoes.
3. Form the mixture into small croquettes.
4. Dip each croquette into the beaten egg, then roll in breadcrumbs to coat.
5. Place the croquettes in the air fryer basket and lightly spray with oil.
6. Cook for 10-12 minutes, or until golden brown and crispy, turning halfway through.
7. Serve warm with a dipping sauce.

Nutritional Information:
- **Calories: 100**
- **Protein: 5g**
- **Fat: 3g**
- **Carbohydrates: 12g**
- **Fibre: 2g**

Meat Recipes

Serves 2

Ingredients:
- 4 pork sausages

Cooking Time: 15 minutes

Instructions:
1. Preheat the air fryer to 180°C.
2. Place the sausages in the air fryer basket.
3. Cook for 12-15 minutes, turning halfway through, until golden brown and cooked through.
4. Serve warm with your favourite sides.

Nutritional Information:
- **Calories: 300**
- **Protein: 15g**
- **Fat: 25g**
- **Carbohydrates: 3g**
- **Fibre: 0g**

Beef and Ale Pie

- Serves 4

Ingredients:
- 500g stewing beef, diced
- 1 onion, chopped
- 1 carrot, diced
- 1 celery stick, diced
- 200ml ale
- 200ml beef stock
- 1 tbsp plain flour
- 1 sheet puff pastry
- 1 egg, beaten
- Salt and pepper to taste
- 2 tbsp vegetable oil

Cooking Time: 20 minutes

Instructions:
1. Preheat the air fryer to 180°C.
2. Heat the oil in a pan, brown the beef, and remove from the pan.
3. Sauté the onion, carrot, and celery until softened.
4. Return the beef to the pan, sprinkle with flour, and cook for 2 minutes.
5. Add the ale and beef stock, and bring to a simmer. Cook for 1 hour, until the beef is tender and the sauce thickens.
6. Transfer the beef mixture to an air fryer-safe dish.
7. Roll out the puff pastry and place it over the beef mixture, trimming any excess.
8. Brush the pastry with beaten egg.
9. Cook in the air fryer for 15-20 minutes, or until the pastry is golden brown.
10. Serve warm.

Nutritional Information:
- **Calories: 500**
- **Protein: 30g**
- **Fat: 30g**
- **Carbohydrates: 25g**
- **Fibre: 2g**

Serves 2

Ingredients:
- 4 lamb chops
- 2 tbsp olive oil
- 1 garlic clove, minced
- Salt and pepper to taste
- 2 tbsp mint sauce

Cooking Time: 12 minutes

Instructions:
1. Preheat the air fryer to 200°C.
2. Rub the lamb chops with olive oil, garlic, salt, and pepper.
3. Place the lamb chops in the air fryer basket.
4. Cook for 10-12 minutes, turning halfway through, until cooked to your liking.
5. Serve with mint sauce.

Nutritional Information:
- **Calories: 400**
- **Protein: 30g**
- **Fat: 30g**
- **Carbohydrates: 3g**
- **Fibre: 0g**

Cornish Pasties

- Serves 4

Ingredients:
- 250g beef skirt, diced
- 1 potato, diced
- 1 onion, finely chopped
- 1 carrot, diced
- 1 sheet of shortcrust pastry
- 1 egg, beaten
- Salt and pepper to taste

Cooking Time: 25 minutes

Instructions:
1. Preheat the air fryer to 180°C.
2. Mix the beef, potato, onion, and carrot in a bowl. Season with salt and pepper.
3. Roll out the pastry and cut into 4 circles.
4. Place a spoonful of the beef mixture onto each pastry circle.
5. Fold the pastry over to form a half-moon shape and press the edges to seal.
6. Brush the tops with beaten egg.
7. Place the pasties in the air fryer basket.
8. Cook for 20-25 minutes, or until golden brown and cooked through.
9. Serve warm.

Nutritional Information:
- **Calories: 450**
- **Protein: 20g**
- **Fat: 25g**
- **Carbohydrates: 35g**
- **Fibre: 4g**

Serves 4

Ingredients:
- 1kg beef roast
- Salt and pepper to taste
- 1 tbsp olive oil
- For Yorkshire Pudding:
- 100g plain flour
- 2 eggs
- 100ml milk
- Pinch of salt

Cooking Time: 50 minutes

Instructions:
1. Preheat the air fryer to 200°C.
2. Rub the beef roast with olive oil, salt, and pepper.
3. Place the roast in the air fryer basket.
4. Cook for 40-50 minutes, or until cooked to your liking.
5. Meanwhile, mix the flour, eggs, milk, and salt to make the Yorkshire pudding batter.
6. After the roast is done, remove it and let it rest. Lower the air fryer temperature to 180°C.
7. Pour the batter into an air fryer-safe dish and cook for 15-20 minutes, until puffed and golden.
8. Serve the roast beef with Yorkshire pudding and your favourite sides.

Nutritional Information:
- Calories: 600
- Protein: 50g
- Fat: 35g
- Carbohydrates: 15g
- Fibre: 1g

- Serves 4

Ingredients:
- 500g pork belly, skin scored
- 1 tbsp olive oil
- 1 tsp sea salt
- 1 tsp fennel seeds

Cooking Time: 40 minutes

Instructions:
1. Preheat the air fryer to 200°C.
2. Rub the pork belly with olive oil, salt, and fennel seeds.
3. Place the pork belly in the air fryer basket, skin side up.
4. Cook for 30-40 minutes, or until the skin is crispy and the meat is tender.
5. Let it rest for 5 minutes before slicing.
6. Serve warm.

Nutritional Information:
- Calories: 450
- Protein: 20g
- Fat: 40g
- Carbohydrates: 0g
- Fibre: 0g

Serves 4

Ingredients:
- 300g beef steak, diced
- 200g lamb kidneys, diced
- 1 onion, finely chopped
- 2 tbsp plain flour
- 100ml beef stock
- 1 sheet suet pastry
- Salt and pepper to taste

Cooking Time: 35 minutes

Instructions:
1. Preheat the air fryer to 180°C.
2. In a bowl, mix the beef, kidneys, onion, flour, salt, and pepper.
3. Roll out the suet pastry and line a pudding basin, leaving enough pastry to cover the top.
4. Fill the basin with the meat mixture and pour in the beef stock.
5. Cover with the remaining pastry and seal the edges.
6. Place the pudding basin in the air fryer basket.
7. Cook for 30-35 minutes, or until the pastry is cooked and the filling is hot.
8. Serve warm.

Nutritional Information:
- **Calories: 500**
- **Protein: 30g**
- **Fat: 30g**
- **Carbohydrates: 25g**
- **Fibre: 2g**

Air Fryer Meatloaf

- Serves 4

Ingredients:
- 500g minced beef
- 1 onion, finely chopped
- 1 egg
- 50g breadcrumbs
- 2 tbsp ketchup
- 1 tbsp Worcestershire sauce
- Salt and pepper to taste

Cooking Time: 30 minutes

Instructions:
1. Preheat the air fryer to 180°C.
2. In a bowl, mix the minced beef, onion, egg, breadcrumbs, ketchup, Worcestershire sauce, salt, and pepper.
3. Shape the mixture into a loaf and place it in an air fryer-safe dish.
4. Cook for 25-30 minutes, or until cooked through and browned on top.
5. Let it rest for 5 minutes before slicing.
6. Serve warm.

Nutritional Information:
- **Calories: 400**
- **Protein: 25g**
- **Fat: 25g**
- **Carbohydrates: 15g**
- **Fibre: 2g**

Air Fryer Bacon-Wrapped Asparagus

Serves 4

Ingredients:
- 12 asparagus spears
- 6 slices of streaky bacon
- Olive oil spray
- Salt and pepper to taste

Cooking Time: 10 minutes

Instructions:
1. Preheat the air fryer to 200°C.
2. Wrap each asparagus spear with half a slice of bacon.
3. Place the bacon-wrapped asparagus in the air fryer basket.
4. Lightly spray with olive oil and season with salt and pepper.
5. Cook for 8-10 minutes, or until the bacon is crispy and the asparagus is tender.
6. Serve warm.

Nutritional Information:
- **Calories: 100**
- **Protein: 6g**
- **Fat: 8g**
- **Carbohydrates: 2g**
- **Fibre: 1g**

Air Fryer Gammon with Pineapple

- Serves 4

Ingredients:
- 4 gammon steaks
- 4 pineapple rings
- 2 tbsp honey
- 1 tsp mustard
- Salt and pepper to taste

Cooking Time: 15 minutes

Instructions:
1. Preheat the air fryer to 200°C.
2. Mix the honey and mustard in a bowl.
3. Season the gammon steaks with salt and pepper.
4. Brush the honey mustard mixture over the gammon steaks.
5. Place the gammon steaks in the air fryer basket.
6. Cook for 10 minutes, then add the pineapple rings on top and cook for another 5 minutes, until the gammon is cooked through and the pineapple is caramelised.
7. Serve warm.

Nutritional Information:
- **Calories: 350**
- **Protein: 30g**
- **Fat: 15g**
- **Carbohydrates: 20g**
- **Fibre: 2g**

Serves 4

Ingredients:
- 500g chicken breast, cut into bite-sized pieces
- 150g plain yogurt
- 2 tbsp tikka masala paste
- 1 tbsp lemon juice
- 1 tsp ground cumin
- 1 tsp ground coriander
- 1 tsp paprika
- Salt and pepper to taste
- Fresh coriander leaves, chopped (for garnish)

Cooking Time: 18 minutes

Instructions:
1. In a bowl, mix together the yogurt, tikka masala paste, lemon juice, ground cumin, ground coriander, paprika, salt, and pepper.
2. Add the chicken pieces to the marinade and coat well. Let it marinate for at least 1 hour, preferably overnight.
3. Preheat the air fryer to 180°C.
4. Place the marinated chicken pieces in the air fryer basket in a single layer.
5. Cook for 15-18 minutes, turning halfway through, until the chicken is cooked through and slightly charred.
6. Garnish with chopped fresh coriander leaves before serving.
7. Serve hot with naan bread or rice.

Nutritional Information:
- **Calories: 250**
- **Protein: 30g**
- **Fat: 8g**
- **Carbohydrates: 10g**
- **Fibre: 1g**

Roast Chicken with Sage and Onion Stuffing

- Serves 4

Ingredients:
- 1 whole chicken (about 1.5kg)
- 1 onion, finely chopped
- 2 garlic cloves, minced
- 1 tbsp fresh sage leaves, chopped
- 100g breadcrumbs
- Salt and pepper to taste
- 2 tbsp olive oil

Cooking Time: 60 minutes

Instructions:
1. Preheat the air fryer to 180°C.
2. In a bowl, mix together the onion, garlic, sage, breadcrumbs, salt, and pepper to make the stuffing.
3. Stuff the cavity of the chicken with the stuffing mixture.
4. Rub the outside of the chicken with olive oil and season with salt and pepper.
5. Place the chicken in the air fryer basket breast side down.
6. Cook for 30 minutes, then turn the chicken breast side up and cook for another 25-30 minutes, or until the chicken is cooked through and golden brown.
7. Let the chicken rest for 10 minutes before carving.
8. Serve hot with roasted vegetables.

Nutritional Information:
- **Calories: 350**
- **Protein: 30g**
- **Fat: 20g**
- **Carbohydrates: 10g**
- **Fibre: 1g**

Serves 4

Ingredients:
- 300g chicken breast, diced
- 2 leeks, sliced
- 1 onion, finely chopped
- 200ml chicken stock
- 150ml double cream
- 1 tbsp plain flour
- 1 sheet puff pastry
- 1 egg, beaten
- Salt and pepper to taste
- 1 tbsp olive oil

Cooking Time: 25 minutes

Instructions:
1. Preheat the air fryer to 180°C.
2. Heat the olive oil in a pan and sauté the onion until soft.
3. Add the chicken and cook until browned.
4. Add the leeks and cook for another 5 minutes.
5. Stir in the flour and cook for 1 minute.
6. Gradually add the chicken stock and cream, stirring continuously until thickened.
7. Transfer the mixture to an air fryer-safe dish.
8. Roll out the puff pastry and place it over the dish, trimming any excess.
9. Brush the pastry with beaten egg.
10. Cook in the air fryer for 20-25 minutes, or until the pastry is golden brown and cooked through.
11. Serve hot.

Nutritional Information:
- **Calories: 400**
- **Protein: 25g**
- **Fat: 25g**
- **Carbohydrates: 20g**
- **Fibre: 2g**

Air Fryer Duck Breast with Orange Sauce

- Serves 2

Ingredients:
- 2 duck breasts
- Salt and pepper to taste
- For Orange Sauce:
- Juice and zest of 2 oranges
- 2 tbsp honey
- 1 tbsp soy sauce
- 1 garlic clove, minced
- 1 tsp cornflour (cornstarch) mixed with 1 tbsp water

Cooking Time: 17 minutes

Instructions:
1. Preheat the air fryer to 180°C.
2. Score the skin of the duck breasts and season with salt and pepper.
3. Place the duck breasts in the air fryer basket skin side down.
4. Cook for 10 minutes, then turn and cook for another 5-7 minutes, or until the duck is cooked to your liking.
5. Meanwhile, prepare the orange sauce: In a saucepan, combine the orange juice, zest, honey, soy sauce, and garlic. Bring to a simmer.
6. Stir in the cornflour mixture and cook until thickened.
7. Slice the duck breasts and serve with the orange sauce drizzled over the top.

Nutritional Information:
- **Calories: 400**
- **Protein: 25g**
- **Fat: 30g**
- **Carbohydrates: 15g**
- **Fibre: 1g**

Serves 4

Ingredients:
- 4 chicken breasts
- 100g butter, softened
- 2 garlic cloves, minced
- 2 tbsp fresh parsley, chopped
- Salt and pepper to taste
- 100g breadcrumbs
- 1 egg, beaten
- Oil spray

Cooking Time: 25 minutes

Instructions:
1. Preheat the air fryer to 180°C.
2. In a bowl, mix together the softened butter, garlic, parsley, salt, and pepper.
3. Cut a slit in each chicken breast to form a pocket.
4. Stuff each chicken breast with the garlic butter mixture.
5. Dip each chicken breast in beaten egg, then coat with breadcrumbs.
6. Place the chicken breasts in the air fryer basket.
7. Lightly spray with oil.
8. Cook for 20-25 minutes, or until the chicken is cooked through and the breadcrumbs are golden brown.
9. Serve hot.

Nutritional Information:
- **Calories: 450**
- **Protein: 30g**
- **Fat: 25g**
- **Carbohydrates: 20g**
- **Fibre: 1g**

Turkey and Cranberry Sausage Rolls

Makes 12 sausage rolls

Ingredients:
- 500g turkey mince
- 100g breadcrumbs
- 1 onion, finely chopped
- 2 tbsp cranberry sauce
- 1 tsp dried sage
- Salt and pepper to taste
- 1 sheet puff pastry
- 1 egg, beaten
- Oil spray

Cooking Time: 17 minutes

Instructions:
1. Preheat the air fryer to 180°C.
2. In a bowl, mix together the turkey mince, breadcrumbs, onion, cranberry sauce, dried sage, salt, and pepper.
3. Roll out the puff pastry and cut it in half lengthways.
4. Spoon the turkey mixture along the centre of each pastry strip.
5. Roll up the pastry to enclose the filling and press to seal.
6. Cut each roll into smaller pieces.
7. Place the sausage rolls in the air fryer basket.
8. Brush with beaten egg and lightly spray with oil.
9. Cook for 15-18 minutes, or until the pastry is golden brown and the filling is cooked through.
10. Serve warm.

Nutritional Information:
- **Calories: 150**
- **Protein: 10g**
- **Fat: 8g**
- **Carbohydrates: 10g**
- **Fibre: 1g**

Serves 4

Ingredients:
- 1kg chicken wings
- 2 tbsp olive oil
- 3 tbsp piri piri sauce
- Salt and pepper to taste
- Lemon wedges (for serving)

Cooking Time: 25 minutes

Instructions:
1. Preheat the air fryer to 200°C.
2. In a bowl, toss the chicken wings with olive oil, piri piri sauce, salt, and pepper.
3. Place the chicken wings in the air fryer basket in a single layer.
4. Cook for 20-25 minutes, shaking the basket halfway through, until the chicken wings are crispy and cooked through.
5. Serve hot with lemon wedges.

Nutritional Information:
- Calories: 350
- Protein: 25g
- Fat: 25g
- Carbohydrates: 5g
- Fibre: 1g

Chicken and Mushroom Risotto

- Serves 4

Ingredients:
- 300g chicken breast, diced
- 200g Arborio rice
- 1 onion, finely chopped
- 200g mushrooms, sliced
- 1.2 litres chicken stock
- 100ml white wine (optional)
- 50g grated Parmesan cheese
- 2 tbsp olive oil
- Salt and pepper to taste

Cooking Time: 12 minutes

Instructions:
1. Preheat the air fryer to 180°C.
2. Heat the olive oil in a pan and sauté the onion until soft.
3. Add the chicken and cook until browned.
4. Stir in the mushrooms and cook for another 5 minutes.
5. Add the Arborio rice and cook for 1 minute.
6. Gradually add the chicken stock, stirring continuously until the rice is cooked and creamy.
7. Stir in the white wine (if using) and Parmesan cheese.
8. Transfer the risotto to an air fryer-safe dish.
9. Cook in the air fryer for 10-12 minutes, stirring halfway through, until heated through.
10. Serve hot.

Nutritional Information:
- Calories: 400
- Protein: 25g
- Fat: 15g
- Carbohydrates: 40g
- Fibre: 3g

Chicken and Ham Hock Terrine

Serves 6-8

Ingredients:
- 300g chicken thighs, diced
- 200g ham hock, shredded
- 1 onion, finely chopped
- 2 garlic cloves, minced
- 1 tsp dried thyme
- 1 tbsp Dijon mustard
- 2 eggs
- 100ml double cream
- Salt and pepper to taste

Cooking Time: 50 minutes

Instructions:
1. Preheat the air fryer to 180°C.
2. In a food processor, blend together the chicken thighs, ham hock, onion, garlic, thyme, Dijon mustard, eggs, double cream, salt, and pepper until smooth.
3. Transfer the mixture to an air fryer-safe terrine dish.
4. Cover the dish with foil.
5. Place the terrine dish in the air fryer basket.
6. Cook for 45-50 minutes, or until the terrine is set and cooked through.
7. Remove from the air fryer and let it cool completely before slicing.
8. Serve chilled with crusty bread or salad.

Nutritional Information:
- Calories: 300
- Protein: 20g
- Fat: 20g
- Carbohydrates: 5g
- Fibre: 1g

Air Fryer Butter Chicken

- Serves 4

Ingredients:
- 500g chicken thighs, diced
- 1 onion, finely chopped
- 2 garlic cloves, minced
- 1 tbsp ginger, minced
- 1 tsp ground turmeric
- 1 tsp ground cumin
- 1 tsp ground coriander
- 1/2 tsp chilli powder (adjust to taste)
- 200ml passata (strained tomatoes)
- 150ml double cream
- 2 tbsp butter
- Fresh coriander leaves, chopped (for garnish)
- Salt and pepper to taste

Cooking Time: 20 minutes

Instructions:
1. Preheat the air fryer to 180°C.
2. In a pan, melt the butter and sauté the onion, garlic, and ginger until softened.
3. Add the diced chicken thighs and cook until browned.
4. Stir in the ground turmeric, cumin, coriander, and chilli powder, cooking for 1 minute.
5. Pour in the passata and simmer for 10 minutes, until the sauce thickens.
6. Stir in the double cream and season with salt and pepper.
7. Transfer the butter chicken to an air fryer-safe dish.
8. Cook in the air fryer for 15-20 minutes, stirring halfway through, until the chicken is cooked through.
9. Garnish with chopped fresh coriander leaves before serving.
10. Serve hot with rice or naan bread.

Nutritional Information:
- Calories: 400
- Protein: 30g
- Fat: 25g
- Carbohydrates: 10g
- Fibre: 2g

Fish and Chips

- Serves 4

Ingredients:
- 4 cod fillets
- 3 large potatoes, cut into chips
- 100g plain flour
- 100ml beer (or sparkling water)
- 1 tsp baking powder
- Salt and pepper to taste
- Oil spray
- Lemon wedges (for serving)

Cooking Time: - 25 minutes for chips - 15 minutes for fish

Instructions:
1. Preheat the air fryer to 200°C.
2. Pat the cod fillets dry and season with salt and pepper.
3. In a bowl, mix the flour, baking powder, and a pinch of salt. Gradually add the beer (or sparkling water) to create a batter.
4. Dip the cod fillets into the batter, coating them evenly.
5. Place the chips in the air fryer basket and spray lightly with oil. Cook for 20-25 minutes, shaking halfway through.
6. Place the battered cod fillets in the air fryer basket. Cook for 12-15 minutes, turning halfway through, until golden and crispy.
7. Serve hot with lemon wedges and tartare sauce.

Nutritional Information:
- **Calories: 400**
- **Protein: 30g**
- **Fat: 10g**
- **Carbohydrates: 50g**
- **Fibre: 5g**

Prawn Tempura

- Serves 4

Ingredients:
- 500g prawns, peeled and deveined
- 100g plain flour
- 1 egg
- 100ml cold sparkling water
- Salt to taste
- Oil spray

Cooking Time: 10 minutes

Instructions:
1. Preheat the air fryer to 200°C.
2. In a bowl, mix the flour and a pinch of salt. In a separate bowl, beat the egg and mix in the cold sparkling water.
3. Combine the flour mixture with the egg mixture to create a batter.
4. Dip the prawns into the batter, coating them evenly.
5. Place the battered prawns in the air fryer basket and spray lightly with oil.
6. Cook for 8-10 minutes, turning halfway through, until the prawns are crispy and golden.
7. Serve hot with dipping sauce.

Nutritional Information:
- **Calories: 200**
- **Protein: 20g**
- **Fat: 5g**
- **Carbohydrates: 15g**
- **Fibre: 1g**

- Serves 4

Ingredients:
- 4 salmon fillets
- 1 sheet puff pastry
- 100g cream cheese
- 2 tbsp fresh dill, chopped
- 1 lemon, zest and juice
- Salt and pepper to taste
- 1 egg, beaten

Cooking Time: 18 minutes

Instructions:
1. Preheat the air fryer to 180°C.
2. In a bowl, mix the cream cheese, dill, lemon zest, and juice. Season with salt and pepper.
3. Roll out the puff pastry and cut into 4 equal pieces.
4. Spread the cream cheese mixture on each piece of pastry.
5. Place a salmon fillet on top of the cream cheese mixture and fold the pastry over to enclose the salmon.
6. Brush the pastry with beaten egg.
7. Place the salmon parcels in the air fryer basket.
8. Cook for 15-18 minutes, until the pastry is golden and the salmon is cooked through.
9. Serve hot with a side salad.

Nutritional Information:
- **Calories: 450**
- **Protein: 30g**
- **Fat: 25g**
- **Carbohydrates: 25g**
- **Fibre: 2g**

- Serves 4

Ingredients:
- 500g squid rings
- 100g plain flour
- 1 tsp paprika
- Salt and pepper to taste
- Oil spray
- Lemon wedges (for serving)

Cooking Time: 12 minutes

Instructions:
1. Preheat the air fryer to 200°C.
2. In a bowl, mix the flour, paprika, salt, and pepper.
3. Coat the squid rings in the flour mixture.
4. Place the coated squid rings in the air fryer basket and spray lightly with oil.
5. Cook for 10-12 minutes, shaking halfway through, until crispy and golden.
6. Serve hot with lemon wedges and a dipping sauce.

Nutritional Information:
- **Calories: 200**
- **Protein: 20g**
- **Fat: 5g**
- **Carbohydrates: 15g**
- **Fibre: 1g**

Fishcakes with Tartare Sauce

- Serves 4

Ingredients:
- 400g white fish fillets, cooked and flaked
- 300g potatoes, boiled and mashed
- 1 lemon, zest and juice
- 2 tbsp fresh parsley, chopped
- 1 egg, beaten
- 100g breadcrumbs
- Salt and pepper to taste
- Oil spray
- For Tartare Sauce:
- 4 tbsp mayonnaise
- 1 tbsp capers, chopped
- 1 tbsp gherkins, chopped
- 1 tbsp fresh parsley, chopped
- 1 tsp lemon juice

Cooking Time: 15 minutes

Instructions:
1. Preheat the air fryer to 180°C.
2. In a bowl, mix the flaked fish, mashed potatoes, lemon zest, lemon juice, and parsley. Season with salt and pepper.
3. Shape the mixture into patties.
4. Dip each patty into the beaten egg, then coat with breadcrumbs.
5. Place the fishcakes in the air fryer basket and spray lightly with oil.
6. Cook for 12-15 minutes, turning halfway through, until golden and crispy.
7. For the tartare sauce, mix all the sauce ingredients in a bowl.
8. Serve the fishcakes hot with the tartare sauce.

Nutritional Information:
- **Calories: 300**
- **Protein: 25g**
- **Fat: 10g**
- **Carbohydrates: 30g**
- **Fibre: 3g**

Grilled Mackerel

- Serves 4

Ingredients:
- 4 mackerel fillets
- 1 lemon, zest and juice
- 2 tbsp olive oil
- 1 tsp paprika
- Salt and pepper to taste
- Fresh parsley, chopped (for garnish)

Cooking Time: 10 minutes

Instructions:
1. Preheat the air fryer to 180°C.
2. In a bowl, mix the lemon zest, lemon juice, olive oil, paprika, salt, and pepper.
3. Brush the mackerel fillets with the lemon mixture.
4. Place the mackerel fillets in the air fryer basket.
5. Cook for 8-10 minutes, until the fish is cooked through and the skin is crispy.
6. Garnish with chopped parsley.
7. Serve hot with a side salad.

Nutritional Information:
- **Calories: 250**
- **Protein: 20g**
- **Fat: 15g**
- **Carbohydrates: 5g**
- **Fibre: 1g**

Smoked Haddock Kedgeree

- Serves 4

Ingredients:
- 300g smoked haddock fillets
- 200g basmati rice
- 1 onion, finely chopped
- 2 garlic cloves, minced
- 1 tbsp curry powder
- 100g peas
- 2 boiled eggs, chopped
- 2 tbsp fresh parsley, chopped
- 1 lemon, cut into wedges
- 2 tbsp butter
- Salt and pepper to taste

Cooking Time: 12 minutes

Instructions:
1. Preheat the air fryer to 180°C.
2. Cook the basmati rice according to package instructions.
3. In a pan, melt the butter and sauté the onion and garlic until softened.
4. Add the curry powder and cook for 1 minute.
5. Add the cooked rice, peas, and smoked haddock fillets (flaked) to the pan. Mix well.
6. Transfer the mixture to an air fryer-safe dish.
7. Cook in the air fryer for 10-12 minutes, until heated through.
8. Stir in the chopped boiled eggs and fresh parsley.
9. Serve hot with lemon wedges.

Nutritional Information:
- **Calories: 400**
- **Protein: 30g**
- **Fat: 15g**
- **Carbohydrates: 40g**
- **Fibre: 3g**

Scallops with Lemon Butter

- Serves 4

Ingredients:
- 12 large scallops
- 2 tbsp butter
- 1 lemon, zest and juice
- 2 garlic cloves, minced
- Salt and pepper to taste
- Fresh parsley, chopped (for garnish)

Cooking Time: 8 minutes

Instructions:
1. Preheat the air fryer to 180°C.
2. In a small pan, melt the butter and add the garlic, lemon zest, and lemon juice. Season with salt and pepper.
3. Brush the scallops with the lemon butter mixture.
4. Place the scallops in the air fryer basket.
5. Cook for 6-8 minutes, until the scallops are cooked through and slightly golden.
6. Garnish with chopped parsley.
7. Serve hot.

Nutritional Information:
- **Calories: 200**
- **Protein: 20g**
- **Fat: 10g**
- **Carbohydrates: 5g**
- **Fibre: 1g**

- Serves 4

Ingredients:
- 400g crab meat
- 100g breadcrumbs
- 1 egg, beaten
- 1 red chilli, finely chopped
- 2 spring onions, finely chopped
- 1 lemon, zest and juice
- 2 tbsp mayonnaise
- Salt and pepper to taste
- Oil spray

Cooking Time: 15 minutes

Instructions:
1. Preheat the air fryer to 180°C.
2. In a bowl, mix the crab meat, breadcrumbs, beaten egg, red chilli, spring onions, lemon zest, lemon juice, mayonnaise, salt, and pepper.
3. Shape the mixture into patties.
4. Place the crab cakes in the air fryer basket and spray lightly with oil.
5. Cook for 12-15 minutes, turning halfway through, until golden and crispy.
6. Serve hot with a dipping sauce.

Nutritional Information:
- **Calories: 250**
- **Protein: 20g**
- **Fat: 10g**
- **Carbohydrates: 20g**
- **Fibre: 2g**

Monkfish Bites

- Serves 4

Ingredients:
- 500g monkfish, cut into bite-sized pieces
- 100g plain flour
- 1 egg, beaten
- 100g breadcrumbs
- 1 lemon, zest and juice
- Salt and pepper to taste
- Oil spray

Cooking Time: 12 minutes

Instructions:
1. Preheat the air fryer to 180°C.
2. Season the monkfish pieces with lemon zest, lemon juice, salt, and pepper.
3. Coat the monkfish pieces in flour, then dip in beaten egg, and coat with breadcrumbs.
4. Place the monkfish bites in the air fryer basket and spray lightly with oil.
5. Cook for 10-12 minutes, turning halfway through, until golden and crispy.
6. Serve hot with a dipping sauce.

Nutritional Information:
- -- **Calories: 200**
- **Protein: 25g**
- **Fat: 5g**
- **Carbohydrates: 15g**
- **Fibre: 1g**

Sweet Treats

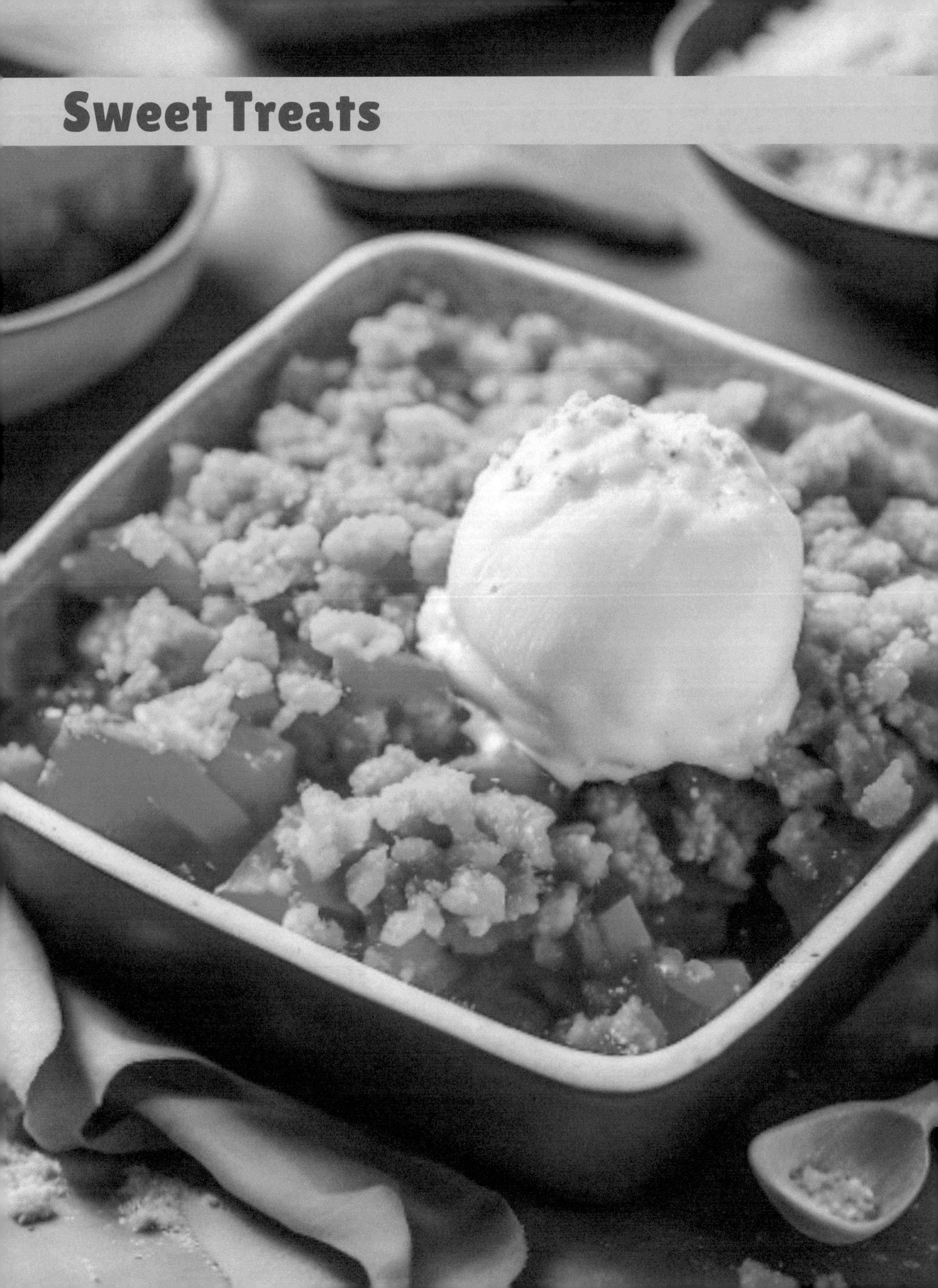

- Serves 4

Ingredients:
- 4 large Bramley apples, peeled, cored, and sliced
- 2 tbsp caster sugar
- 1 tsp ground cinnamon
- 150g plain flour
- 100g unsalted butter, chilled and cubed
- 75g demerara sugar

Cooking Time: 25 minutes

Instructions:
1. Preheat the air fryer to 180°C.
2. In a bowl, mix the sliced apples with caster sugar and cinnamon. Transfer to an air fryer-safe dish.
3. In another bowl, rub the flour and butter together until it resembles breadcrumbs.
4. Stir in the demerara sugar and sprinkle the crumble mixture over the apples.
5. Place the dish in the air fryer and cook for 20-25 minutes, until the topping is golden brown and the apples are tender.
6. Serve warm with custard or ice cream.

Nutritional Information:
- **Calories: 300**
- **Protein: 3g**
- **Fat: 12g**
- **Carbohydrates: 45g**
- **Fibre: 4g**

Lemon Drizzle Cake

Serves 8

Ingredients:
- 200g self-raising flour
- 200g caster sugar
- 200g unsalted butter, softened
- 4 eggs
- Zest of 2 lemons
- Juice of 1 lemon
- 100g icing sugar

Cooking Time: 35 minutes

Instructions:
1. Preheat the air fryer to 160°C.
2. In a bowl, beat together the butter and caster sugar until light and fluffy.
3. Gradually add the eggs, one at a time, beating well after each addition.
4. Fold in the self-raising flour and lemon zest.
5. Pour the batter into an air fryer-safe cake tin.
6. Cook for 30-35 minutes, or until a skewer inserted into the centre comes out clean.
7. While the cake is baking, mix the lemon juice with icing sugar to make the drizzle.
8. Once the cake is done, poke holes in the top with a skewer and pour over the lemon drizzle.
9. Allow to cool in the tin before serving.

Nutritional Information:
- **Calories: 350**
- **Protein: 5g**
- **Fat: 20g**
- **Carbohydrates: 40g**
- **Fibre: 1g**

Makes 6 tarts

Ingredients:
- 1 sheet ready-made shortcrust pastry
- 100g raspberry jam
- 100g ground almonds
- 100g caster sugar
- 100g unsalted butter, softened
- 2 eggs
- 50g plain flour
- Flaked almonds (for topping)

Cooking Time: 20 minutes

Instructions:

1. Preheat the air fryer to 180°C.
2. Roll out the pastry and cut into circles to fit in air fryer-safe tart tins.
3. Spread a thin layer of raspberry jam over the base of each pastry case.
4. In a bowl, cream together the butter and caster sugar.
5. Beat in the eggs one at a time, then fold in the ground almonds and flour.
6. Spoon the almond mixture over the jam in each tart tin.
7. Sprinkle with flaked almonds.
8. Place the tarts in the air fryer and cook for 15-20 minutes, until golden brown.
9. Allow to cool before serving.

Nutritional Information:
- **Calories: 300**
- **Protein: 5g**
- **Fat: 20g**
- **Carbohydrates: 25g**
- **Fibre: 2g**

Air Fryer Chocolate Fondants

Makes 4 fondants

Ingredients:
- 100g dark chocolate
- 100g unsalted butter, plus extra for greasing
- 100g caster sugar
- 2 eggs
- 2 egg yolks
- 100g plain flour
- Cocoa powder (for dusting)

Cooking Time: 12 minutes

Instructions:

1. Preheat the air fryer to 200°C.
2. Grease air fryer-safe ramekins with butter and dust with cocoa powder.
3. Melt the chocolate and butter together in a heatproof bowl over a pan of simmering water.
4. In another bowl, whisk together the eggs, egg yolks, and caster sugar until pale and thick.
5. Fold in the melted chocolate mixture, then sift in the flour and fold until combined.
6. Divide the mixture between the ramekins.
7. Place the ramekins in the air fryer and cook for 10-12 minutes, until the edges are set but the centre is still gooey.
8. Serve immediately with a dusting of icing sugar or a scoop of vanilla ice cream.

Nutritional Information:
- **Calories: 400**
- **Protein: 6g**
- **Fat: 28g**
- **Carbohydrates: 30g**
- **Fibre: 2g**

Serves 6

Ingredients:
- 150g self-raising flour
- 75g suet
- 50g caster sugar
- 100g currants
- Zest of 1 lemon
- 100ml milk
- 1 tsp ground cinnamon

Cooking Time: 40 minutes

Instructions:
1. Preheat the air fryer to 180°C.
2. In a bowl, mix together the flour, suet, caster sugar, currants, lemon zest, and ground cinnamon.
3. Gradually add the milk, mixing until it forms a soft dough.
4. Shape the dough into a log and wrap in baking paper, then in foil.
5. Place the wrapped dough in the air fryer basket.
6. Cook for 35-40 minutes, until cooked through and risen.
7. Allow to cool slightly before unwrapping and slicing.
8. Serve warm with custard.

Nutritional Information:
- **Calories: 250**
- **Protein: 4g**
- **Fat: 10g**
- **Carbohydrates: 35g**
- **Fibre: 2g**

Air Fryer Shortbread

Makes 12 pieces

Ingredients:
- 150g plain flour
- 100g unsalted butter, chilled and cubed
- 50g caster sugar, plus extra for sprinkling

Cooking Time: 15 minutes

Instructions:
1. Preheat the air fryer to 160°C.
2. In a bowl, rub together the flour and butter until it resembles breadcrumbs.
3. Stir in the caster sugar and knead until it forms a dough.
4. Roll out the dough on a lightly floured surface to about 1cm thickness.
5. Cut into desired shapes and place in the air fryer basket.
6. Cook for 12-15 minutes, until the shortbread is pale golden.
7. Sprinkle with extra caster sugar and allow to cool on a wire rack.

Nutritional Information:
- **Calories: 100**
- **Protein: 1g**
- **Fat: 6g**
- **Carbohydrates: 12g**
- **Fibre: 0.5g**

Serves 8

Ingredients:
- 1 sheet ready-made shortcrust pastry
- 400g golden syrup
- 150g fresh breadcrumbs
- Zest and juice of 1 lemon
- 1 egg, beaten

Cooking Time: 25 minutes

Instructions:
1. Preheat the air fryer to 180°C.
2. Roll out the pastry and line an air fryer-safe tart tin.
3. In a bowl, mix together the golden syrup, breadcrumbs, lemon zest, lemon juice, and beaten egg.
4. Pour the mixture into the pastry case.
5. Place the tart in the air fryer and cook for 20-25 minutes, until the filling is set and the pastry is golden.
6. Allow to cool before serving.

Nutritional Information:
- **Calories: 300**
- **Protein: 3g**
- **Fat: 10g**
- **Carbohydrates: 50g**
- **Fibre: 1g**

Serves 8

Ingredients:
- 200g mixed dried fruit
- 100g unsalted butter, softened
- 100g dark brown sugar
- 2 eggs
- 150g plain flour
- 1 tsp baking powder
- 1 tsp mixed spice
- 50ml milk

Cooking Time: 40 minutes

Instructions:
1. Preheat the air fryer to 160°C.
2. In a bowl, cream together the butter and dark brown sugar.
3. Beat in the eggs one at a time.
4. Fold in the flour, baking powder, and mixed spice.
5. Stir in the mixed dried fruit and milk until well combined.
6. Pour the mixture into an air fryer-safe cake tin.
7. Cook for 35-40 minutes, or until a skewer inserted into the centre comes out clean.
8. Allow to cool before slicing.

Nutritional Information:
- **Calories: 300**
- **Protein: 4g**
- **Fat: 12g**
- **Carbohydrates: 45g**
- **Fibre: 2g**

Serves 4

Ingredients:

- 500g rhubarb, chopped
- 100g caster sugar
- 1 tsp ground ginger
- 150g plain flour
- 100g unsalted butter, chilled and cubed
- 75g demerara sugar

Cooking Time: 25 minutes

Instructions:

1. Preheat the air fryer to 180°C.
2. In a bowl, mix the rhubarb with caster sugar and ground ginger. Transfer to an air fryer-safe dish.
3. In another bowl, rub the flour and butter together until it resembles breadcrumbs.
4. Stir in the demerara sugar and sprinkle the crumble mixture over the rhubarb.
5. Place the dish in the air fryer and cook for 20-25 minutes, until the topping is golden brown and the rhubarb is tender.
6. Serve warm with custard or ice cream.

Nutritional Information:

- **Calories: 300**
- **Protein: 3g**
- **Fat: 12g**
- **Carbohydrates: 45g**
- **Fibre: 4g**

Serves 8

Ingredients:

- 200g digestive biscuits, crushed
- 100g unsalted butter, melted
- 1 tin condensed milk (397g)
- 3 bananas, sliced
- 300ml double cream, whipped
- Grated chocolate (for garnish)

Cooking Time: 35 minutes (plus chilling time)

Instructions:

1. Preheat the air fryer to 160°C.
2. Mix the crushed digestive biscuits with melted butter and press into an air fryer-safe dish to form a base.
3. Place the condensed milk in a shallow dish, cover with foil, and cook in the air fryer for 30-35 minutes until it turns into caramel.
4. Pour the caramel over the biscuit base and chill in the fridge for 1 hour.
5. Arrange the banana slices over the caramel layer.
6. Spread the whipped cream on top and garnish with grated chocolate.
7. Chill for another hour before serving.

Nutritional Information:

- **Calories: 450**
- **Protein: 4g**
- **Fat: 30g**
- **Carbohydrates: 45g**
- **Fibre: 2g**

Makes 20 gingerbread men

Ingredients:

- 350g plain flour
- 1 tsp bicarbonate of soda
- 2 tsp ground ginger
- 1 tsp ground cinnamon
- 125g unsalted butter
- 175g dark brown sugar
- 1 egg
- 4 tbsp golden syrup

Cooking Time: 10 minutes

Instructions:

1. Preheat the air fryer to 170°C.
2. In a bowl, sift together the flour, bicarbonate of soda, ground ginger, and cinnamon.
3. In another bowl, cream together the butter and dark brown sugar.
4. Beat in the egg and golden syrup.
5. Gradually stir in the dry ingredients until it forms a dough.
6. Roll out the dough on a floured surface to about 0.5cm thickness.
7. Cut into gingerbread men shapes and place in the air fryer basket.
8. Cook for 8-10 minutes, until golden brown.
9. Allow to cool before decorating.

Nutritional Information:
- **Calories: 100**
- **Protein: 1g**
- **Fat: 4g**
- **Carbohydrates: 15g**
- **Fibre: 0.5g**

Serves 8

Ingredients:
- 1 sponge cake, cubed
- 1 packet of jelly (as per packet instructions)
- 500ml custard
- 300ml double cream, whipped
- Fresh berries (for garnish)
- Flaked almonds (for garnish)

Cooking Time: No cooking required, but requires chilling time.

Instructions:

1. Prepare the jelly as per packet instructions and let it set in the fridge.
2. Layer the cubed sponge cake in an air fryer-safe dish.
3. Pour the jelly over the sponge cake layer and chill in the fridge until set.
4. Pour the custard over the set jelly and sponge cake layer.
5. Spread the whipped cream on top.
6. Garnish with fresh berries and flaked almonds.
7. Chill for at least 1 hour before serving.

Nutritional Information:
- **Calories: 350**
- **Protein: 5g**
- **Fat: 20g**
- **Carbohydrates: 35g**
- **Fibre: 2g**

Makes 12 cakes

Ingredients:
- 200g self-raising flour
- 100g unsalted butter, chilled and cubed
- 75g caster sugar
- 100g mixed dried fruit
- 1 egg
- 2 tbsp milk
- 1 tsp vanilla extract

Cooking Time: 12 minutes

Instructions:
1. Preheat the air fryer to 180°C.
2. In a bowl, rub together the flour and butter until it resembles breadcrumbs.
3. Stir in the caster sugar and mixed dried fruit.
4. Beat together the egg, milk, and vanilla extract, then add to the dry ingredients.
5. Mix until it forms a stiff dough.
6. Drop spoonfuls of the dough onto a piece of baking paper in the air fryer basket.
7. Cook for 10-12 minutes, until golden brown.
8. Allow to cool on a wire rack before serving.

Nutritional Information:
- **Calories: 150**
- **Protein: 2g**
- **Fat: 6g**
- **Carbohydrates: 22g**
- **Fibre: 1g**

Air Fryer Welsh Cakes

Makes 12 cakes

Ingredients:
- 225g self-raising flour
- 100g unsalted butter, cubed
- 75g caster sugar
- 50g currants
- 1 egg
- 2 tbsp milk
- 1 tsp mixed spice

Cooking Time: 10 minutes

Instructions:
1. Preheat the air fryer to 180°C.
2. In a bowl, rub together the flour and butter until it resembles breadcrumbs.
3. Stir in the caster sugar, currants, and mixed spice.
4. Beat together the egg and milk, then add to the dry ingredients.
5. Mix until it forms a dough.
6. Roll out the dough on a floured surface to about 1cm thickness.
7. Cut into rounds and place in the air fryer basket.
8. Cook for 8-10 minutes, until golden brown.
9. Allow to cool before serving.

Nutritional Information:
- **Calories: 150**
- **Protein: 2g**
- **Fat: 6g**
- **Carbohydrates: 22g**
- **Fibre: 1g**

Conclusion

Encouragement for Beginners

Embarking on a culinary journey with the Ninja Double Stack Air Fryer can be both exciting and intimidating, especially for beginners. However, it is important to remember that cooking is an art that can be mastered with practice, patience, and a bit of creativity. The Ninja Double Stack Air Fryer is designed to make this process easier and more enjoyable.

Here are some words of encouragement for those just starting out:

Start Simple: Begin with easy and straightforward recipes to get a feel for the air fryer's capabilities. Simple dishes like chips, roasted vegetables, or basic chicken recipes are perfect for familiarising yourself with the appliance.

Learn and Experiment: Don't be afraid to experiment with different ingredients and cooking times. The Ninja Double Stack Air Fryer is versatile, and with time, you'll discover new ways to use it to create delicious meals. Each attempt is a learning experience that brings you closer to mastering the appliance.

Follow Instructions: While it's great to experiment, following the instructions in this cookbook, especially for the first few tries, can help you achieve the best results. Understanding the basics will give you the confidence to tweak recipes to your liking.

Be Patient: Cooking with an air fryer might be different from traditional methods you are used to. Patience is key. Give yourself time to adjust and learn the nuances of the appliance.

Celebrate Small Wins: Every successful dish, no matter how simple, is a win. Celebrate your achievements and share your creations with family and friends. Their positive feedback can be a great motivator.

Join a Community: There are many online communities and forums where Ninja Double Stack Air Fryer users share tips, recipes, and experiences. Joining these communities can provide support, inspiration, and troubleshooting advice.

Don't Get Discouraged: Not every recipe will turn out perfect the first time. If a dish doesn't meet your expectations, analyze what went wrong and try again. Persistence is key to becoming a proficient air fryer cook.

Have Fun: Remember, cooking should be enjoyable. Have fun experimenting with flavors and textures. The more you enjoy the process, the more rewarding it will be.

Final Thoughts

The Ninja Double Stack Air Fryer is more than just a kitchen gadget; it is a tool that can transform the way you cook and eat. It offers a healthier, quicker, and more efficient way to prepare a wide variety of dishes. By following the recipes and tips in this cookbook, you can unlock the full potential of your air fryer and create meals that are both delicious and nutritious.

Cooking with the Ninja Double Stack Air Fryer has numerous benefits. Its ability to cook with little to no oil makes it an excellent choice for those looking to reduce their fat intake without sacrificing flavor. The versatility of the appliance means you can prepare everything from breakfast to dessert, all with one device. Its efficiency saves you time in the kitchen, allowing you to focus on other important aspects of your life.

Moreover, the Ninja Double Stack Air Fryer is an environmentally friendly option, consuming less energy than traditional ovens. Its compact size and rapid cooking technology contribute to a lower carbon footprint, making it a sustainable choice for eco-conscious cooks.

As you continue to explore the recipes in this cookbook, you will gain confidence in your cooking skills and discover new ways to use your air fryer. The wide range of dishes available means you can cater to various tastes and dietary preferences, making meal planning easier and more enjoyable.

This cookbook is designed to inspire and guide you on your culinary journey with the Ninja Double Stack Air Fryer. Whether you are a seasoned cook or a beginner, the recipes and tips provided will help you create meals that are not only delicious but also healthy and convenient.

For Your Notes

For Your Notes

For Your Notes

For Your Notes

For Your Notes

For Your Notes

For Your Notes

For Your Notes

For Your Notes

For Your Notes

For Your Notes

For Your Notes

For Your Notes

For Your Notes

For Your Notes

For Your Notes

For Your Notes

For Your Notes

For Your Notes

Made in United States
Troutdale, OR
12/06/2024